LIVING WITH
THE SON
IN YOUR
EYES

To Lois,
your love of God
and love of life makes
my heart smile.
Randall Carpenter
10 Nov 2013

RANDALL L. CARPENTER

LIVING WITH THE SON IN YOUR EYES

TATE PUBLISHING
AND ENTERPRISES, LLC

Published by Tate Publishing & Enterprises, LLC
127 E. Trade Center Terrace | Mustang, Oklahoma 73064 USA
1.888.361.9473 | www.tatepublishing.com

Tate Publishing is committed to excellence in the publishing industry. The company reflects the philosophy established by the founders, based on Psalm 68:11,
"The Lord gave the word and great was the company of those who published it."

Book design copyright © 2013 by Tate Publishing, LLC. All rights reserved.
Cover design by Arjay Grecia
Interior design by Jomar Ouano
Author's image photographed by Jay Anne Boza, www.bozartz.com
   Author's contact information:
      Randall L. Carpenter, RanCath Writings, 10620 Eagle's View Drive, Knoxville, TN 37922. (865) 254-7405

Published in the United States of America

ISBN: 978-1-62854-937-9
1. Religion / Christian Life / General
2. Religion / Christian Life / Devotional
13.10.22

DEDICATION

This book is dedicated to the pastors and staff of Cokesbury Church, a United Methodist community of faith located at 9908 Kingston Pike, Knoxville, TN 37922, in appreciation for their leadership and dedication to Cokesbury Church, the kingdom of God, and the least, the last, and the lost of Knox County and the City of Knoxville.

CHURCH MISSION STATEMENT

"Loving people into a relationship with Jesus Christ to change the world."

Former Senior Minister: Dr. G. Steven Sallee
Senior Minister: Rev. Stephen B. DeFur
Associate Minister: Dr. Kenny Faught
Minister of Discipleship: Rev. Rebekah P. Fetzer
Director of Recovery Ministeries: Rev. Mark Beebe
Former Associate Minister: Rev. Micah Nicolaus
Former Associate Minister: Rev. Jason Gattis
Director of Music: Dr. Marcelo Urias

CONTENTS

FOREWORD

Throughout my life, I have relied on my faith in God and His continuous grace and mercy to guide my steps. I have strived, with many falls, to make my life an example of my faith. Though I find it increasingly difficult at times not to be of this world, I have tried to keep my focus and love for God. Being a follower of Jesus Christ has helped me when I have been tempted to retaliate against an injustice or close my eyes and let this world lead me. Maybe I could have been more successful had I done what others around me did or had I been willing to compromise my beliefs for the sake of a paycheck. Maybe I would have received fame and fortune had I just been more agreeable to turn my head and look the other way, but I didn't. Maybe a better way of saying it is not that I didn't, but more accurately, I couldn't.

Within this book, I hope you will read words that will inspire you, challenge you, and make you more secure in your faith.

Being a Christian is more than going to church, it is more than reading your Bible, and it is more than feeling good about yourself because you profess to be a Christian. God knows our heart. He knows our thoughts and our actions.

When we act like a Christian on Sunday but live like the devil throughout the week, we are not fooling anyone, especially God. Live your life as if it is a Bible that others are reading. You can say all the right words and sing all the right songs, but if your life is an example of the exact opposite, it will only confuse those who are watching you.

God sent His Son to teach us what we need to know about being a Christian. Every answer to every question is in the Bible, waiting for us to read it. It is my hope that when you read the writings and the devotionals that follow, the words will speak to you and bring you closer to our Lord and Savior. God bless you and may your life be richly blessed.

WITH THE SON IN YOUR EYES

Learning to live life
with the Son in your eyes
means seeing things that others do not see.

Where others see hopelessness,
you see a chance to help.

Where others see only a derelict,
you see a chance to show compassion.

Where others see an opportunity to get ahead,
you see a chance to do the right thing.

Where others use excuses for their cruelty,
you use reasons for your kindness.

When you live life
with the Son in your eyes
you can see more clearly.
Because
when the Son is in your eyes
His love will always light the way.

What does it mean to "live with the Son in your eyes"? It means you do not see what others see. You see what others don't see. You see where you can make a difference for others, not where you can benefit yourself. You see opportunities to do for others, not opportunities to make a name for yourself. Jesus never did anything for Himself. Everything He did was to teach, guide, and set an example for others to follow. Jesus struggled with the injustices around Him. He struggled with the oppression He witnessed. He saw people taking advantage of others. He saw unfairness just as we see it today. He was saddened by what the world had become. That is why God sent Jesus to live on this earth. Is it any different now than then?

What we say, how we say it, how we think, how we react, and how we use our talents for the benefit of others are the definition of living with the Son in your eyes. The way we interpret what we see and the reaction we have to it is our personal testament to living with the Son in your eyes. God sent His Son not to condemn the world but to give us an example to follow.

Following that example is tough; it is not easy. Why would it be any easier for us when it was never easy for Jesus? Living with the Son in your eyes does not mean you stand over people and quote chapter and verse to them. It does not mean you will see and do the right thing all the time. What it does mean is before you make a decision, you will ask yourself if what you are going to do will benefit someone. Will it be detrimental to others or you? Is it something you should do, not because you can, but because it is the right thing to do? And lastly, as a Christian, if no one sees you do this, will it matter?

God does not expect us to live pious lives. He does not expect us to give away all we have or live a life of poverty. What He does expect is a life lived with our eyes open so we can see where we can make a difference. That is all He wants from us: to make a difference by living with the Son in your eyes.

> O Lord, who may abide in your tent? Who may dwell on your holy hill? Those who walk blamelessly, and what is right, and speak the truth from their heart; who do not slander with their tongue, and do no evil to their friends, nor take up a reproach against their neighbors; in whose eyes the wicked are despised, but who honor those who fear the Lord; who stand by their oath even to their hurt; who do not lend money at interest, and do not take a bribe against the innocent. Those who do these things shall never be moved.

> Psalm 15:1–5

Twenty Rules to Live Your Life By

November 18, 1967

To my children,

At the present time, I wish I could say something that you, children, could use to carry you through life. But I can't think of a thing except to always live your lives with all you have.

1. Never lose faith in God.
2. Be honest with yourself and others.
3. Always speak the truth.
4. Live up to your obligations and promises.
5. Do not drink intoxicating liquors.
6. Remember that good character is above all things.
7. If someone entrusts you with a secret or confides in you, never betray them.
8. Keep yourself innocent of any wrongdoing.
9. When you speak to a person, look him straight in the face.

10. Always maintain a cheerful outlook on life. Stay as happy as you are now.
11. Connie, avoid temptation through fear you may not withstand it.
12. Your character cannot be injured (essentially) except by your own acts.
13. If anyone speaks evil of you, let your own life be such that no one will believe any bad of you.
14. Always be active both physically and mentally.
15. Never forget to be kind to others.
16. Work hard and be competitive, but play by the rules.
17. There are unkind people in the world who are jealous, envious, etc., of you. Don't let them worry you. Ignore them.
18. Get a good education and make a good name for yourself in whatever you do. Be the best you know how.
19. Don't let other people drag you down.
20. Anything worth doing is worth doing well.

I don't think I need to tell you anymore than you already know. Always be good to your mother and make her proud of you. Also remember that I will always be counting on you to do exactly as if I was still with you.

I love all of you with eternal love,
Daddy

Years ago my father, W. Howard Carpenter, before he had his first open-heart operation, wrote this letter to me and my brothers and sister titled "Twenty Rules to Live Your Life By." We knew nothing about the letter until the day after he passed away.

I found it in four envelopes, addressed separately to me, Rick, Jack, and Connie, on May 3, 2001, the day after our dad passed away. It has become one of our most treasured possessions.

What if you died tomorrow? Would your wife, husband, children, brother, or sister know how you feel about them? Don't wait. Leave something behind that God will surely bless: your love.

> Hear, my child, your father's instruction, and do not reject your mother's teaching; for they are fair garland for your head, and pendants for your neck. My child, if sinners entice you, do not consent.
>
> Proverbs 1:8–10

> My child, do not walk in their way; keep your foot from their paths; for their feet run to evil, and they hurry to shed blood.
>
> Proverbs 1:15–16

A Quiet Stream

Quietly we sit
on the bank of a stream
listening to the birds sing,
watching the water carry the ducks by
and hearing the wind whisper
a melody of solace.
For a time we are nowhere else
For a moment our mind empties
And for eternity we will never
forget this moment in our life.
The rustling of the leaves
as the wind passes through
reminds us of a rain shower.
The sunbeams striking the ground
make a palette of colors,
illuminating brightly all around us
and creating shadows
we enter and leave as we walk.
Suddenly we realize,
nowhere but here
can we imagine
we would rather be.
Moments like these
are so few in our lives.

Capture them when you can.
Hold them in your heart.
One day you will remember this moment
and with fondness you will reflect upon it.
A memory is a precious thing.
With it you can always go back
and live this moment again and again and again.

There are times in our life when being alone is really what we need. We must take time to be by ourselves and get away from all the pressures we endure every day. The stress of work, the demands of family, the fear of not knowing what to do if a crisis in our life were to happen, the fear of losing a relationship that means everything to us, and even the contemplation of our own insignificance can be very stressful. All of these are legitimate reasons to need time alone. But it takes more than just being by ourselves. It takes more than just "getting away from it all." What it really takes to be by yourself and be making a difference is when you incorporate prayer in those moments alone. A prayer of thanksgiving, a prayer for forgiveness, a prayer for understanding and strength will make your time alone more meaningful. When you sincerely pray from your heart and don't let your mind get in the way, you feel the power of the prayer. We have all begun a prayer of need and suddenly found ourselves thinking of something else. During our prayer we said something in our mind that triggered a thought and suddenly we were no longer asking God for what we were praying about.

Take a moment before you pray and clear your mind. Close your eyes, visualize the darkness around you and the void the darkness has created. Now, begin your prayer and try to see every word you say, feel the emotion of every word, and search in that darkness until your mind can do nothing but concentrate on the words you are saying. When you become focused on the words your heart is expressing, then you are truly alone with God and you are making a difference in your life.

> So I tell you, whatever you ask for in prayer, believe
> that you have received it, and it will be yours.
>
> Mark 11:24

A Slow Walk

A slow walk
down the country roads of our life
teach us many things.
The brightness of the sunlight
casts faceless shadows on the ground,
proving our existence,
but displaying nothing more,
and telling us it is our responsibility
to color out the blackness.
The feel of a summer breeze
swaying the grass and trees
pushes its formless self past us
and disappears somewhere around us,
just like many people we encounter
as we walk through life.
The beauty of the mountains
towering majestically above us
reminds us there are obstacles
we must face in our life
in order to get to where we need to go.
A slow walk
down the country roads of our life
gives us time to think,
to ponder, to reflect

but most importantly,
to appreciate all that God has given us.
Each step we take in life
is either a step forward or a step back.
Life is meant to be enjoyed.
Take your time
and look around you.
The country roads of your life are waiting.
Find one and embrace its healing power.
You will never be the same
and your heart will be filled with new meaning.

Has there ever been a time in your life when you felt you were burning the candle at both ends? Has there been a time when at the beginning of the day you could not see how you were going to get everything accomplished, but you did? We have all gone through these times. With the growing demands of this world and the stresses that accompany just getting through each day, being busy is just a part of life. As difficult as it may be, we must learn to slow to a walk. We must learn to slow down enough to appreciate what we have and what God has placed around us. His world is beautiful. The people within it are His creation. We must learn to make friendships and nurture them. We must take each day and find within it moments of grace for ourselves. We must find moments when we can reflect and appreciate what God has created in us and around us. This world is one country road after another if we just slow our pace, open our eyes, open our heart, and let God walk beside us.

> Sing to him, sing praises to him, tell of all his wonderful works. Glory in his holy name; let the hearts of those who seek the Lord rejoice. Seek the Lord and his strength, seek his presence continually. Remember the wonderful works he has done, his miracles, and the judgments he uttered.
>
> 1 Chronicles 16:9–12

Autumn Songs

With the passing of summer
comes a time of peace and reflection.
The trees begin to sing their lullabies
before they lay down to sleep for the winter.
The beauty of their melodies
shows brightly in their colors
as they compete in perfect harmony
for our attention.
These annual sonnets
are another sign of God's love for us.
As if wrapping His arms around us,
He slows our pace,
and with a sigh of relief
we settle into His arms
and enjoy this concert of love.
God's love surrounds us every day
if we just look and listen.
Please don't miss your melody of love.
It was written with you in mind.

God is so wonderful. He shows us miracles of His work
and examples of His love in the world around us. The sounds
of life are all around us, and we take them for granted. The

colors and the smells engulf us, but we barely notice. There are things we overlook and beauty that we look right through. God is not offended though. He is like a loving father who continually forgives his children's lack of noticing all they have and all he has provided them. Don't let the world around you and the gifts from God pass you by. Savor every moment. Grasp and hold tightly the smallest of memories. For many of us, those memories may be all we may have when someone we love passes away. You are loved so very much by God. Don't forget this, and you will begin to see so much more around you, and precious memories will fill your heart and mind.

> From his fullness we have all received, grace upon grace.
>
> John 1:16

BIG ENOUGH

God, you are big enough to move a mountain
But small enough to live in my heart.
You are big enough to control the tides
But small enough to be a whisper.
You are big enough to spin the earth
But small enough to be a tear.
You are big enough to give rain to our world
But small enough to ride a snowflake from heaven.

God, make me big enough to hear your words
But small enough to see your miracles.
You are God.
I am not.
Make me big enough to remember.

I know this one is a big one for everyone. We all feel like we can handle anything and everything. We go through our lives making one decision after another and never considering the consequences. Then one day, we find ourselves in trouble or we do something to hurt someone we love. We do not know where to turn, so we turn to God for help. We pour out our hearts to Him and promise we will never make another decision without praying about it first. Then we wait and expect a miracle to happen because we have asked for God's forgiveness for not trusting Him. Soon we find ourselves being presented with an answer, and we take full credit for the solution. We forget everything we prayed and everything we promised God.

This is like the grandmother who was walking on the beach with her grandson when a large wave suddenly swept him out of her grasp and into the ocean. Immediately she fell to her knees and prayed to God to return her beloved grandson. She promised to give everything she owns to the church if He would just bring back her grandson. Sure enough, a large wave deposits the little child back on the beach unharmed. Her only response: he had a hat on!

Why do we do this? We do this because we are not big enough to realize we are not God. Don't let yourself become bigger than God. He is in control if you just follow His teachings and accept them.

> Trust in the Lord forever, for in the Lord God you have an everlasting rock.
>
> Isaiah 26:4

EVERY PRAYER

For every prayer,
there is an answer;
For every answer,
there is a reason;
We may not know it.
We may not see it.
But one day,
we will surely live it.

How often do we proclaim that we know God is all-powerful and can do anything but at the same time we don't let Him help us through the trials and tribulations of our life? We pray to Him for help and then forget to wait for His direction. God does not reach down from heaven and take you by the hand and lead you to the answer of every problem, every need, and every desire you may have. But He does hear your prayer and He does answer every prayer. We may not realize this and we may not see the answer, but we can feel certain that He has heard us.

Because we are here on earth, it is our task to show God's love to each other. We are God's children, and the miracles in our life are not our doing. They are the hands of God guiding our thoughts, our actions, and our decisions to make our life a living testimony of His love. Don't be afraid to turn to Him with every need. Also, don't forget to thank Him for everything in your life. God's love is pure, unconditional, and free. Reach out to Him. He is waiting to enter your heart.

> Ask, and it will be given you; search, and you will find; knock, and the door will be opened. For everyone who asks receives, and everyone who searches finds, and for everyone who knocks, the door will be opened.
>
> Matthew 7:7–8

FOR TERESA

The most important things in life
are not the things we touch,
but the things that touch us.
The feeling when your baby
grabs your finger
and grasps your heart
at the same time.
The tears that streak your face
as you watch your child succeed.
The pride in your heart
as you see young men and women
parade by in uniform.
The chills on your skin
when your daughter says,
"I'm pregnant."
These are the important things in life.
The things that let us know we are alive.
God gave us emotions
and through these emotions
our hearts are touched.
Don't be afraid to show your emotions
when something touches you.
It may be just the emotion you need
to change your life forever.

One of the greatest gifts God gave man was the ability to feel emotion. We have the ability to feel happy, sad, and emotionally moved by what we see, hear, and experience. A single tear will streak our face as we watch a child succeed. The pride we feel as we watch a strong, self-assured, and confident young man or woman pass in uniform. The unmistakable and heart-pounding emotion we feel the first time we hold our own child. What would life be like if we could not feel emotion? There would have never been music. There would have never been art, dance, or sports.

Our lives are filled with emotions. It is the purpose for everything we do. We fall in love because of it. We mourn those we lose because of it. We either move forward with our lives because of it or we do not move at all because of it. God gave Adam the ability to feel pain, misery, shame, and guilt when He allowed him to realize his sin in the garden of Eden. When we worship God, we must be able to feel His power; see His miracles; and through the sacrifice of His son, Jesus Christ, feel His pain. God loves us, and we must show Him our love by living a Christian life every day.

Without emotions, we would only hear and never comprehend, we would read our Bible and not know where to apply its teaching in our life, and we would see but never appreciate. Without emotions, we do not exist.

Embrace your emotions. Let them bring you joy; let them bring you sadness; let them help you worship. God is always with you, and He is giving you signs of His existence. Believing without seeing is called faith. You do not have to see God to know He is there. You can feel it every day if you just allow Him into your heart.

> Although you have not seen him, you love him; and even though you do not see him now, you believe in him and rejoice with an indescribable and glorious joy, for you are receiving the outcome of your faith, the salvation of your souls.

> 1 Peter 1:8-9

GOD'S FAVORITE WORDS

God's favorite words are "I Will."

I will
…love you forever
…forgive your every sin
and listen when you speak.
I will
…wait for you.
I will
…give you comfort
…be happy when you are happy
and be sad when you are sad.
I will
…cry when you cry.
I will
…know your every need
…pick you up when you are down
and watch over you every day.
I will
…whisper in your ear.
I will
…talk to you if you listen
…help you know right from wrong.
I will
…always be here for you.

God knows you and needs you
as much as you need Him.
Be not afraid
because He is a God of second chances.
It is never too late to seek Him
because His favorite words are "I will."

Where else in your life can you find someone who will always say to you "I will?" Someone who promises to never leave you no matter what you do. Someone who is never more than a single word of need away from you. Someone who wants you to want and need Him and is always waiting for the opportunity to help you through whatever you are enduring. God is truly seeking a committed relationship with you. He cares for you and your relationship with Him more than the things you have accomplished in this world. He is seeking from you a committed relationship that is not one-sided. If you trust in God and trust in His words, He will always be there because you know He will always be there. Trust God. He trusts you.

> Go therefore and make disciples of all nations, baptizing them in the name of the Father and of the Son and of the Holy Spirit, and teaching them to obey everything that I have commanded you. And remember, I am with you always, to the end of the age.

Matthew 28: 19-20

GOD'S HANDS

God,
I feel your hands all around me.
I feel your hands upon my head
comforting me.
I feel my face cupped between your hands
as you speak softly to me.
I feel your hands gently on my back
giving me encouragement.
I feel your hands beneath my chin
helping me hold my head up.
And
I feel your hands lifting me
from my despair.
Please, never let me go, God.
And let it be your hands I clasp
every time I pray.

Have you ever noticed how important the hands are? Everything we do physically involves our hands. They help us hold a glass of liquid that will quench our thirst. They help us hold on to tools that will be used to build a shelter. Some people use their hands to produce income to make their life better. They grasp the hands of our children so they are safe and do not get lost, and they allow us to hold the ones we love and let them know they are special.

Our hands are also important to God. They are clasped when we pray. They are open to receive gifts that God bestows on us, and they help fight off anything that comes between us and God.

God's hands are important to us. They are the hands that His Son, Jesus Christ, had nailed to the cross at Calvary. God's hands are the ones we use to pick up those who have fallen. God's hands are the ones we wrap our hands around each time we fold them in prayer.

Your hands are God's hands if you believe in His Son, Jesus Christ. When you are doing your work with God's hands, there is nothing you cannot accomplish.

> Now may our Lord Jesus Christ himself and God of our Father, who loved us and through grace gave us eternal comfort and good hope, comfort your hearts and strengthen them in every good work and word.
>
> 2 Thessalonians 2:16–17

How Much He Loved Me

I turned to the Lord one day
and I asked Him how much He loved me.
He looked at me and with arms spread widely
He said, "I love you this much, my son."
Not understanding, I asked,
"But how much is that, my Lord?"
Once again, His arms spread widely, He said,
"I love you this much, my child."
"But, Lord", I said.
"Don't you know any other way of showing me?"
"I know no better way of showing you
than the way in which I am."
"How about a priceless gift
or a trip to show me how much you love me?"
Once again the Lord looked at me and said,
Gesturing as before,
"I love you this much, my son.
I have but this single way of showing you."
Not yet grasping what my Lord was saying,
I begged for Him to tell me more.
But my Lord just looked up at me
and with arms spread widely,
as He had shown me before,
He lay down on that cross
and showed me how much He loved me.

What does the word *sacrifice* mean to you? Does it mean giving up your tickets to a ball game so a friend can go? Does it mean not going out to dinner a couple of times a week so you can save enough money to take a vacation? Is it a sacrifice if you agree to let your kids have the television so they can watch their favorite show? I suppose in this world, those would be considered sacrifices. But what if someone told you, "I want you to agree to leave your home. Go to a place where everyone will question everything you do. You will have to try to convince everyone who sees you or hears you that if they follow you, their life will be better. You will be falsely judged due entirely to fear and prejudice, and one of the people you trust most will betray you and you will know it but do nothing about it. Then after enduring all that, you will be tried, convicted and sentenced to death, all in one day. But your accusers will only kill you if the people you were sent to teach choose you to die over a thief. Sadly, the people you love will turn their backs on you and allow you to be put to death in the most painful way possible."

Now, would you call that a sacrifice? How about if you were asked to send your only son to endure all this? Could you do that? God sent His only Son, Jesus Christ to be abused, accused, and misunderstood. Why would He do that? Quite simply, because the world needed an example to have as a guide so man would change his evil ways. Have we changed? I am not sure. It seems the only time most people turn to

God is when there is a disaster in the world or in their own life. God loves us no matter what, this is for sure. But do we love Him no matter what? This is a question we must ask ourselves. How would you answer that question?

> For God so loved the world that he gave his only Son, so that everyone who believes in him may not perish but may have eternal life.
>
> John 3:16

I Sometimes Forget

The Lord is my shepherd each passing day
I strive to do His will.
Though faithful as I think I am
I sometimes grow too still.

I sometimes forget to say hello
to a person who needs a smile.
I sometimes forget to reach out to others
and hold them for a while.

I sometimes forget to pray at night
or even pray at all.
I sometimes forget that friend of mine
the one I need to call.

I sometimes think of only me
and the problems I have to bear.
I sometimes forget Your love so pure
and my burdens I know You share.

Now help me, Lord, to remember all
the things I know to do.
The things that cost nothing to give
but bring me close to you.

As Christians, we sometimes forget the very foundation of our faith is to show others the love of Jesus Christ. We forget to reach out to God to help us get through our days. We fail to say a prayer of thanks for all we have in our lives. We all have a tendency not to realize what we have. We fail to see for ourselves, until something happens around us, that our lives are richly blessed. Our ability to see, to hear, to walk, and to speak are blessings from God, and we take them for granted. We look around us and realize we live in a safe neighborhood. We drive a car and arrive safely where we are going. We watch our children go off to school and know they will be safe until they return to us.

So much have we overlooked and looked over when it comes to the blessings in our life. God placed His only child, Jesus Christ on this earth to teach and guide us. God loved us so much that after His Son had finished His teachings, He allowed him to be crucified for our sins. He did this to show us the sacrifice He was willing to make to show us He loves us.

God does not ask for much. He asks that we worship one God and minister to others about His love for them.

Enduring life's pains and miseries is nothing compared to the pain His Son endured on the cross. We worship a God of love, a God of forgiveness, and a God of second chances. It is never too late to know God personally. You just need to accept His love and believe in Him with all your heart. The best part is you can do it right now where you are, and He will hear your prayer of forgiveness.

> All the prophets testify about him that everyone who believes in him receives forgiveness of sins through his name.
>
> Acts 10:43

SITTING ON OUR SUITCASE

Sometimes in life
we find ourselves sitting on our suitcase.
We feel alone and abandoned.
We feel lost and scared
and we hear the darkness
all around us.
We cry out
and our voice fades into the night.
We stare into the abyss
looking for a glimpse of light to follow.
We reach out,
hoping to grasp something
to pull ourselves forward.
But
all our cries for help
seem to drift away like an echo.
When you feel alone,
you are not.
When you can see no path,
there is one.
God is always there.
You are never alone.
Just believe.
His hand is always extended to you.

How many times have we all been in this situation? We are lost and looking for a place to go and hide. How many times have we found ourselves staring into our own abyss? We are waiting for someone to come for us or for someone to show us the way out. We have all been there and we never want to return. The fear we felt was real. It was overpowering and crippling. Our mind raced years ahead, and we saw misery. Our mind looked back, and we saw where we came from but cannot go back. Maybe it was a divorce. Maybe it was a broken home or a time in our life where our fears were so great they paralyzed us.

What we didn't realize was God was there. He was watching and waiting for us to hear His whispers, feel His hand, or see the path He was laying out for us. It could have been that small voice we heard in our mind when we stopped talking and everything was silent. It could have been that feeling of solitude we suddenly felt when we realized a way out or a better understanding of the pain we were feeling.

When we become a Christian, it does not mean bad things will not happen to us. What it does mean is we will have someone we can turn to when we feel sad, depressed, or lost. It also means we will have someone we can speak to when we are happy and content. We realize we are not alone when we feel the pains and strife of this world. I think what happens too often is that no one else has ever experienced what we have gone through. They have, and they made it. You too can do the same if you trust in God. Let Him ease your burden and show His love for you. God wants us to be happy. I am sure it makes God happy when we are happy. Look for a way to be happy.

> He who rescued us from so deadly a peril will continue to rescue us; on Him we have set our hope that he will rescue us again.
>
> 2 Corinthians 1:10

REACHING

In life we spend our time
reaching up, reaching down, or reaching out.
When we choose to reach down,
we do so to either offer a hand of compassion
or a hand to hold someone down.
When we choose to reach up,
we do so to either recognize God's presence
or to push away everyone around us.
But when we choose to reach out,
this is when we show our true character.
Then we do so to offer a hand of comfort
or we do so to take something from someone.
How you choose to reach up, down, or out
may seem unimportant.
But how you do so
tells others who you are.
How far you can reach
is not a measurement of distance,
but more accurately a measure of influence.
Doing the right thing
is not always the easiest thing to do,
but it is still the right thing.

We spend most of our lives trying to reach for things. We reach for things that physically exist like food and clothing. We reach for things that emotionally exist like love and friendship. And we reach for things that are not here now but we are working toward, like a college degree or owning a home. Though our life is filled with moments where we are looking forward to obtain a goal, our greatest success in reaching will be when we reach out to others and make their lives better.

God provides us opportunities to display our love for people every day. When those opportunities present themselves, it is how we respond to them that will let us know if our heart and mind work together. Everyone, no matter who they are, feels compassion. What we do when we feel compassion is what separates one person from another. When you see a person in need, do you first think something negative about them, or do you look for an opportunity to help? When a situation presents itself to take advantage of someone, are you tempted to do so, or do you avoid the temptation and make sure no one else does it either? How we think and how we act can be two entirely different things. We may say to ourselves, "I need to do something about that," but we don't.

Why do we do this? We know if we did respond, it would be the right thing to do, but we don't. Sometimes we think if we responded, we would be obligated to continue giving.

Logic tells us we cannot take care of every problem in the world. We cannot take care of everyone, and we should not. But there are people and situations that we come across every day that, with a little effort on our part, we could have a positive influence on.

The best way to make a difference in someone's life and those around them is to be a good Christian example. That can be your daily hand-up to someone who is looking for a new direction. People who have a Christian heart look for the right things to do. When Jesus Christ walked on this earth, His reach went much further than the extension of His arms. His teachings and examples have reached all the way around the world. All He asks us to do is take His hand and reach out to others, so they can take our hand and reach out to others and so on until eventually His love will find its way back to Him. What you do with your life is what you give back to God. Make it count.

> Finally, all of you, have unity of spirit, sympathy, love for one another, a tender heart, and a humble mind. Do not repay evil for evil or abuse for abuse; but, on the contrary repay with a blessing. It is for this you are called—that you might inherit a blessing.
>
> 1 Peter 3:8–9

ROOMS IN OUR HEART

Quietly we sit and listen.

Listening to what we think is our mind
reminding us of times gone by.
The feelings, the dreams,
the remembering
are not from our mind;
they are doors opening in our heart.

Our heart has many rooms.
Some filled with sad memories,
others filled with happy ones.
But
deep within our heart
lay tiny chambers
where single memories are stored.

Single memories of chance encounters,
glances from someone we never met
but will never forget.
Smells, sounds, scenes, or feelings

that happened only once
but have burned themselves indelibly
into our heart and soul.

We never know these memories are there.
We don't even realize they are being stored
until one day,
a door opens to one of these tiny rooms
and the memory that passes through
stops us but for a moment
to reflect on a time gone by.

Someone, something, someplace
remembered with fondness so real
you feel almost taken back to that time
to live it once again.

Why do we have these rooms in our heart?
Because
they store memories we must never forget.
Memories that teach us, remind us, help us
or keep someone close to us
whom we will never forget.

The rooms in our heart
are there in each of us.
The key to unlocking each of them

is but a moment away,
waiting in life to be experienced,
and opened widely
to bring to life yet again
a memory we need today.

This writing has been shared with many people who have suffered the loss of someone they loved. Many people have requested a copy, and it has been sent all over the United States. I hope after you read this you realize there are memories in your life that live in tiny rooms in your heart. God loves us enough to leave behind a little of everyone we have loved and of special times that have been in our life. May your memories be good ones and your rooms open widely.

Life is made up of many pictures, events, and encounters that we remember but don't realize we remember. We take vacations, go on day trips, and go about our days watching, seeing, and experiencing people, places, and things. We cannot remember everything, but we do remember the most important things. These are the immediate memories we can recall at any time and do so in vivid detail. Most of those memories are wonderful, and we love sharing them with others. Unfortunately, we also possess memories that brought sadness to our life. These are unavoidable and, hopefully, are not the majority of your memories.

Our heart is a wonderful thing. It has an endless capacity to store memories—memories that we don't even know are there. We go through life and see, hear, and even smell things that leave an impression upon us. People, places, pictures, words, sounds, and, yes, even smells can burn themselves indelibly into our heart. Why they do so, we have no idea. Our heart stores them away in tiny rooms where they stay until we need them. We need them because they remind us of who we are, where we came from, and who we left behind that we will never forget. We use these memories to teach us not to make the same mistakes again. We use these memories to remind us that someone loved us once even if we feel no one loves us now.

God is at work every day in our lives. He gives us everything we need to make our life what we want it to be. Sometimes our life does not turn out the way we want, but we always have God to talk to. We also have our memories to guide us, teach us, or remind us of times gone by. Maybe that is all we need to make our days ahead better.

> Beloved, let us love one another, because love is from God; everyone who loves is born of God and knows God. Whoever does not love does not know God, for God is love. God's love was revealed among us in this way: God sent his only Son into the world so we might live through him. In this is love, not that we loved God but that he loved us and sent his Son to be the atoning sacrifice for our sins.

> 1 John 4:7–12

SACRED MEMORIES

Within every heart
there is a place we store memories.
Memories of people we have met in our life.
Those memories may remind us every day of that person
or they may only bring them to mind occasionally.
Then there are those special memories,
memories that are so sacred,
and almost always private,
that burn in our heart and mind for years.
They give us life,
and they make us long for someone
who will make our life complete.
Do not give up on those sacred, precious memories.
God knows your heart,
your hopes,
and your desires.
Life is sometimes the road we must travel
that eventually brings us to the one we were always meant for.
Do not let your past
keep you from recognizing your future.
Happy endings do exist
when two hearts truly love each other.

There are times in our life that we must live in order for us to end up where we should have been all along. It could be a marriage to someone we thought we loved or thought loved us. It could be moving away and leaving someone behind we knew we loved but could never tell. We have these times in our life, and only by the grace of God do we get a chance to return to who or what we left. Your heart has a longer memory than your mind. You push out the thoughts of someone else because you feel guilt or because the pain of remembering is just too difficult. You fill your life with things that take the space but never seem to take the place of that one you realize was meant by God to be with you. Your lonely heart only gets lonelier until one day it quits feeling anything. That is when your life turns upside down. It has nothing to do with who you are with or if they love you or not. It has everything to do with those sacred memories that are in your heart. What you see in front of you cannot replace what you feel inside of you. We have all felt this loneliness. Sometimes all we have left is to know God is love and He loves you.

> No testing has overtaken you that is not common to everyone. God is faithful, and he will not let you be tested beyond your strength, but with the testing he will also provide the way out so that you may be able to endure it.
>
> 1 Corinthians 10:13

THE ELEVENTH COMMANDMENT

When you feel your world
falling down around you,
remember the eleventh commandment:
thou shalt hangeth in there.
When you know it is going to hurt
to do or say what needs to be done,
remember the eleventh commandment:
thou shalt hangeth in there.
When no word or friend
can take away the pain and suffering,
remember the eleventh commandment:
thou shalt hangeth in there.
God loves us.
And through Him
nothing is impossible.
So remember the eleventh commandment
because
God has great things planned for you.
And because of His love for you,
God also
hangeth in there.

Life is tough; it's that simple. We struggle every day with the things this world throws at us. We struggle to make a living. We struggle to protect our children from things we know will harm them. We struggle with our marriage, our relationships, and our sense of right and wrong. We make decisions every day without a clue if they are right. We feel ourselves hanging by a thread and know eventually that thread will break or we will not be able to hang on any longer. Is this you? I know it is me. I learned and follow the eleventh commandment—thou shalt hangeth in there.

God sent His Son to this earth and did not give Him any special treatment. Jesus endured the pains and miseries of those times. I am sure He had worries. He felt pain, if not for Himself then for all those around Him. I am sure He worried about food and shelter, if not for Himself, then for His disciples. He worried about the relationships He had with others, and He was perplexed why He could not make others believe all that He was telling them.

Sometimes we cannot do any more than just hang in there. Worries are part of being of this world. God did not promise us if we follow Him we will be worry-free. Actually, it is quite the opposite. When you become a Christian, you see the world differently. The problems around you become more glaring, and you want to help, but sometimes you cannot. The best we can do at those times is just hang in there with the confidence and assurance that we are not alone because God also "hangeth in there."

Now to him who by the power at work within us is able to accomplish abundantly far more than all we can ask or imagine, to him be glory in the church and in Christ Jesus to all generations, forever and ever. Amen

Ephesians 3: 20-21

THE MEASURE OF A MAN

The measure of a man
is not the strength in his arms,
but the compassion in his heart.
It is not the time
he spends making money,
but the time he spends
making a difference.
It is not the length of his footsteps
that will make him great,
but the hesitation in his stride
when he encounters someone in need.
No,
the measure of a man
is not just looking for the next thing to do,
but more importantly,
looking for the next right thing to do,
then having the strength to do it.

This writing is especially precious to me. It is one that I did for my son, Ryan. I wrote this after having lunch with Ryan and his fiancé, Cassie. At lunch, we were discussing whether being physically strong made you a man. Ryan brought this up because, quite frankly, he is very physically strong. Listening to him convey his feelings on being able to lift certain weights or being able to move certain things others could not gave me an opportunity to teach him the real measure of a man. When he finished talking, God gave me this simple response: "It is not the strength in your arms that will make you a man but the compassion in your heart." The answer took him by surprise, and he just sat thinking about what I had said. It must have meant something to him because he didn't say a word; he just sat there.

God teaches us that compassion for others and doing His work is what He wants us to do. We sometimes must assert ourselves, but we can do so without being cruel. The difference we make in this world will be our legacy when we are gone. What we did and how we did it will be the dash on our tombstone between our birth date and our date of death. Being a man does not require intimidation or power or tests of physical strength. Being a man is more a measure of the distance of your influence. Did you bring someone along with you as you followed Christ's teachings? Did you live a life that others could see Christ in you and knew your life made a difference?

Christ was a man in every sense of the word. Like a verse from a song I heard many years ago, "He was tough as nails." I think a better phrasing of that verse would have been, "He was tougher than nails." What is the measure of a man? It is what you do in your life for those you love and those you have yet to meet.

How does God's love abide in anyone who has the world's goods and sees a brother or sister in need and yet refuses help?

1 John 3:17

TOUCH OF SILENCE

The touch of silence on my heart
is soft and gentle.
It is soothing and tranquil
and it draws emotion from my soul.
It brings to the surface vulnerability.
It brings to the open single solutions
but also creates more unanswerable questions.
The touch of silence on my mind
is challenging and competitive.
It is inquisitive but measureable.
Measureable to the point of a beginning and an end.
The touch of silence on my life
is a touch of need, of want, and of desire.
It allows me to ponder and reflect.
It allows me to reach inside of myself
and pull to the surface
feelings I thought I had long forgotten.
I treasure silence in my life.
It sounds so beautiful at times.
Its touch can be everlasting.
Its touch so relinquishing.
For it's the touch of silence
that leaves a lasting impression.
An impression you will never forget.
An impression that will change you completely.

Silence in our lives is a vital part of our growth. It is then that we see things more clearly. It is then that we sometimes discover we have gone from a problem to a solution. Being by yourself, away from distractions, can renew your mind. It can allow you to release the air you hold inside out of fear that your insecurities will be discovered. Silence can be the best form of healing. It can be the one thing your life needs. It can be all you may need to renew your spirit to face the things you are forced to endure. Seek out a place where you can hear nothing but the silence around you. When you do so, then close your eyes and enjoy the moments. When we pray, we become silent. This allows us to listen and focus on the prayer we are hearing or the prayer we are saying. When there is silence, we comprehend better. The noises and distractions stop for just a moment as if out of reverence.

Do not be afraid of the touch of silence. Its touch is soothing and embracing. It will bring solace to your spirit and comfort to your soul. It does so when you allow it to engulf you. You allow it to surround and embody you. Silence is our means of escape. When you enjoy moments of silence, you are not abandoning those you love. You are not walking away from your responsibilities. You are, in fact, doing the exact opposite. You're giving yourself a moment of peace and that is what even Christ would do many times. God wants us to enjoy our life. He wants us to know we are loved. Taking time to enjoy the silence brings us closer to Him. God speaks to us in our times of silence when we are paying the closest attention. Enjoy your moments of silence. In them, you will understand the healing powers of the touch of silence.

> Peace I leave with you; my peace I give to you. I do not give to you as the world gives. Do not let your heart be troubled, and do not let them be afraid.
>
> John 14:27

THE TOUCH OF YOUR HAND

God,
with every touch of your hand,
I feel your love and power
changing my heart
and changing my life.
With every touch of your hand
my soul is refreshed
and my hopes are renewed.
Your love for me
has no boundaries
and I know with you in my life
I can accomplish anything.
God, take my hand in yours
and lead me so I may follow.
In you I trust.
In you I believe.
And in your name
I will lead others.
Not by my words,
but by my actions
and by my examples.

Throughout our lives, there are moments when we know God has reached out and touched our life. We know there can be no other explanation why something happened. A car accident avoided at the last moment, and we had no idea how. A miraculous recovery from death by someone we love when all medical opinions were sure survival was impossible. And the greatest miracle of all, a person coming back from death with a clear memory of where they had been and what they had seen. When this happens the touch of God's hands are felt by everyone they share the experience with. When God allows someone to return to this earth, He does so because their work is not complete. It could be that their family still needed them. It could be that they have not yet made the difference on the earth that God intended them to make. Whatever the reason, God has a purpose and we must follow it.

My father, W. Howard Carpenter, was one of those people God sent back. My father was a devoted Christian, and he lived a Christian life. He raised us to follow the teachings of Jesus Christ, and he did so by his example. However, in 1967, he had a massive heart attack. He was given six months to live. He was required to undergo open heart surgery to save his life. After the surgery, he was in excruciating pain. He could not bear it anymore, and he prayed to God to remove the pain. The next thing he remembered was sitting on the bank of a stream, totally pain-free. He saw the stream flowing by. He felt the breeze on his face, and he heard the song "How Great Thou Art" playing softly around him. As he took it all in, he then heard a voice ask him if he was ready to come. He knew where he was, and he knew what had happened. Without hesitation he said, "No, I want to go back to my family." The next thing he remembered was waking up with a doctor sitting on his chest doing heart massage. He had died. He had been dead for over six minutes due to a blood clot in his femoral artery. He had also been in heaven.

My Dad recovered and went on to have two more open heart operations before he died on May 2, 2001, thirty-four years after he was told he had six months to live. My dad was different after coming back from heaven. He spoke differently, and people listened. People were drawn to him. Strangers would come up to him and ask his advice. God's hands had touched my dad and people felt it. Anyone who ever knew or met my dad knew it. He was a true disciple, and I loved him very much. He was one of God's angels, and he made a difference in countless people's lives, including mine.

> It will not be so among you; but whoever wishes to be great among you must be your servant, and whoever wishes to be first among you must be your slave; just as the Son of Man came not to be served but to serve, and to give his life a ransom for many.
>
> Matthew 20:26–28

WHEN I MISS YOU

When I start to miss you
I just close my eyes
and look into my heart.
You are always there
and I know that is where
I can always find you.
For you are with me, God.
You are beside me always.
I am never without you.
I am never alone
because you are always present
and I feel your arms surround me.
I know no fear.
I feel no absence.
I give you my heart.
I give you my life.
Thank you, God.
Show me the way.

When you truly know God and know that He is with you at all times, it is an amazing feeling. Knowing that God is working in your life is a comfort unlike any other. When God moves into your heart, your life changes. You become a different person, and you think differently. You don't become a meeker person or someone that folds their hands and says, "I understand and forgive you," each time something happens to you. I think you still believe everyone should be accountable for their behavior. Living with God in your heart makes you more prone to see things differently. You don't see the harsh side of things as often as you did. Your life seems more focused as you deal with the temptations of this world. Living a Christian life is not easy. It sometimes puts you at odds with this world. You begin to not look for the next thing to do in your life but, more accurately, the next right thing to do. You may see situations where you know you can help but society says you will be making a mistake if you do. But you decide to do it because it is the right thing to do. This is when you are living a Christian life.

You sometimes will have to do things that will not be in your best interest but would be the right thing to do. That is when you are living with God in your heart.

Do not fear the changes in yourself. Your life will be better for the new path you have chosen. God blesses good deeds. The blessings may not be now, but they will surely be yours.

> Then Jesus said to the Jews who had believed in him, "If you continue in my word, you are truly my disciples; and you will know the truth will make you free."

> John 8:31–32

WHERE I WAS HIDING

You found where I was hiding,
behind so many walls;
I felt you tugging at my heart
in my stumbles and my falls.
I always felt that I was right
and could handle anything,
until I felt a grief so deep
I could not hear you sing.
I have my job, my pride, my wealth,
they've served me all these years;
But nothing made my heart so full
as when I shed those tears.
Tears of joy and tears of life
and tears from deep within,
you helped me find my way to you
and forgave me all my sins;
You held me close and let me know
that we all have things we hide.
But when I gave them all to you
you cast them all aside;
Now take my hand and lead me down
a path you have for me,
I'll walk beside you day to day
and worship only thee.

We have all been where this writing explains. We have all been in a place where we were all alone or felt there was no one who could help us. We put up walls around ourselves to keep everyone out, and we managed to also keep God out. We build these walls around us for many reasons. Most of them are built to protect us. Some of them are built to hide ourselves from others. We try to hide our insecurities. We try to hide our lack of confidence. But sometimes we build these walls because we don't feel we need anyone, and the easiest way to avoid everyone is to build a wall.

We start building our walls by developing a solid foundation of arrogance. We then start laying the bricks of individual prejudices and stupidity. The bricks are held together by mortar made from the hard work of others but claimed entirely by us. Before we know it, there is a wall around us that we feel keeps everyone out and our ego intact. The problem is we start feeling we are in control and everything revolves around us. We feel we are the reason everything and everyone has any worth. We build our wealth and others praise our accomplishments. We are God in our own mind.

The problem is the wealth we have built means nothing because of the way we obtained it. The accolades we hear from people are not actual compliments but are ways to feed our inflated ego and manipulate us. We are not God. We are a wall that is easily scaled and mostly transparent. Everyone can see through us, but no one tells us because no one cares that much about us. That is everyone except, of course, God. He loves us in spite of our arrogance, our pride, and our condescending ways.

One day we realize what has happened to us and our life changes. God is now in charge, and our heart is filled with love, compassion, and benevolence. We become a child of God. This is when real change happens. When we change our heart, our head will follow. We can do this. We can change. Ask God for guidance and then follow it. He is waiting in the shadows right now to change our life. When we do, we will know what true wealth is because we opened our heart and let Him in.

> since all have sinned and fall short of the glory of God; they are now justified by his grace as a gift, through the redemption that is in Christ Jesus.
>
> Romans 3:23–24

WHISPERS FROM GOD

There are whispers from God
that surround us every day.
The final sigh of a baby
as it falls back to sleep.
The rustling of the leaves
as the wind passes through.
The rhythmic melody from the beach
as the ocean rushes back and forth.
The sound of the rain
as it falls from heaven
and brings peace to your heart.
These whispers from God
surround us every day.
Listen and you will hear them.
God loves to whisper
and He speaks in many ways.

The voice of God can be heard every day. His voice can be loud or it can be soft. It can sound like a whisper, just barely audible, or it can be so deafening, it is immeasurable. Listening for the voice of God will make you more appreciative of all He has created. The swaying of the trees as God softly sighs. The roar of a waterfall as it cascades down a mountain side.

The gentle resting of a sunbeam as it lands on your skin and falls asleep.

There are many whispers of God. Can you hear them? Stop and take a moment to listen to the sounds around you. Some are just sounds of life, but others are whispers from God meant only for you. He speaks to us because He loves us. Sometimes it may be through another person's voice, or it may be through a sound we cannot remember hearing before. God whispers to us. Have you heard Him today?

> Listen, and hear my voice; Pay attention, and hear my speech.

Isaiah 28:23

IF

If you fail,
it doesn't mean
you are a failure.
If you stumble,
it doesn't mean
you have fallen.
If you feel no hope,
it doesn't mean
you are hopeless.
God is always with you.
He hears your voice
when you are stressed.
He feels your pain
when you cry for help.
Trust God with all your heart.
You must remember
there is nothing you could ever do
or anything you have ever done
that would make God love you
any more or any less
than He does at this very moment.
Open your heart
and forget your past.
You are loved
and you are forgiven
and it no longer matters.

Making mistakes is part of living your life. We are not perfect, and we will not be perfect until we have ascended into heaven. God does not expect us to be perfect, but He does expect us to realize our mistakes. Even if you think you're just one mistake away from being alone, you are not. As long as you are alive, God is always with you. He is never far away even when you feel you are far away from Him. Forgiving you for your mistakes is not hard for God to do because He loves you. Forgiving yourself for your mistakes is the real challenge. God gives us a mind and a heart. We cannot forget what we have done and those we have hurt. The pain we cause others is always greater than the pain we cause ourselves.

If you could be assured that all the mistakes you have made in your life could be instantly forgiven and you could start anew, would you want that? Of course, you would. God will do that, but you have to accept that it has been done. Do not worry that others will doubt you. People will always doubt you no matter what you have done or not done for many reasons, some of which have nothing to do with you.

Look within your heart and see where you can change. If you do not feel a change is needed then make sure your life is one that benefits others and not solely yourself. God is waiting to enter your heart. Why don't you let Him come in?

There is therefore now no condemnation for those who are in Christ Jesus. For the law of the Spirit of life in Christ Jesus has set you free from the law of sin and of death.

Romans 8:1-2

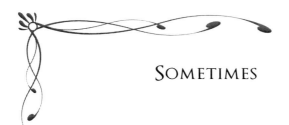

SOMETIMES

Sometimes in life, fair is not what happens.
Sometimes right does not shine through.
Sometimes we don't understand
why we did all the work
and someone else got all the credit.
Sometimes hard work is not enough
and success is not being number one.
Sometimes getting ahead could mean staying behind.
Yes, sometimes in life God doesn't seem fair.
He takes ones we love and seems to leave nothing.
Sometimes in life we strive to understand
and barely manage to be confused.
We must always keep ourselves alert.
We must always be ready for anything.
Sometimes life is not what we want it to be.
Sometimes life is what we least expect
and therefore what we fear the most.

Why isn't life fair? We do what we are supposed to but
seem to get no credit for it. Others make huge mistakes and
are held as examples to everyone else. We hear about how
highly successful people became successful by lying and
cheating and manipulating others. We do not understand

how this seems to happen so often. It appears no one is held accountable for their behavior. Why does this happen?

The reason why is not the answer. The answer is because people make choices and the choices they make determine the life they will live. If you choose to lie and cheat, you may become successful, but no one will trust you. If you choose to manipulate others for your own personal gains, you may obtain a position of authority, but others will never respect you. Throughout our lives, we will experience injustices, unfairness, prejudices, and we will encounter people who do not deserve what they have achieved. It is not our place to judge even if their choices cause us grief.

Throughout our lives, we make thousands of choices without knowing how they will affect our future. How we use those choices in our life will determine if we are successful by the standards of the world or we are successful in the eyes of God. No one is promised fame and fortune unless you are a follower of Jesus Christ. But your fame and fortune will come in heaven and may never come on this earth. Why is life not fair? Only God knows.

> I have hope in God—a hope that they themselves
> also accept—that there will be a resurrection of
> both the righteous and the unrighteous.
>
> Acts 24:15

FEAR NOT

Fear not, for I am with you.
I will never leave you.
I will forever be beside you.
I will walk where you walk.
I will sleep where you sleep.
I will be your shadow
when your days are sunny
and your comforter
when the rains do come.
I am forever near you.
You are my child
as I am your Father.
My heart knows only you
and my life I gave for you.
Fear not, my child
for in me you are always safe.
Take my words
and build your life around them.
They will guide you along your way.
Fear not, for I am with you
because my Father is always with me.

What a wonderful feeling to know God is always with you. He will always be beside you. He will always be there to comfort you. He will always hold you when you are sad and rejoice with you when life brings you happiness. Knowing that God is there no matter what is reason to rejoice. Turning to Him when you are fearful will not make the fear go away, but it will make it easier to endure. God is with us, and we are with Him, no matter when we need Him. He promises to always be there with us. Believe in this, and your life will serve God.

May your every prayer begin with a thank-you to God for all you have been blessed with in your life. May your blessings be ones that you use to glorify God. And may your life be lived in a way that advances the kingdom of God. Amen.

> So we can say with confidence, "The Lord is my helper; I will not be afraid. What can anyone do to me?"
>
> Hebrews 13:6

FOR THOSE WHO FEEL

For those who feel they do not have a prayer,
give them yours;
For those who feel God has abandoned them,
give them hope and assurance;
For those who feel they are at the end of the road,
let them know God's love has no end.
You are the salt and the light.
Share what you have,
what you know,
and what you feel.
God has blessed you
and given you this moment to make a difference.
So much needs to be done
and you have the love to do it.

There is so much pain and suffering in this world. People are looking for an answer to their needs. Even those who love God are wanting to know where He is in their times of need. They feel He has left them when they needed Him most. God would never leave us. He is always with us. He sees our suffering and feels our pain. We know this because He loves us and He shares our pain with us. That is why He places angels on earth to help us.

The angels are not hard to find. They exist all around us. Actually, they exist right at this moment. There is nothing physically special about God's angels. The only difference is not what they know but what they choose to do. If you have seen someone in need and extended a hand of compassion, you have been one of God's angels. If you have felt yourself pulled toward someone you have never met but feel you must speak to, you have been one of God's angels. If you have known the right thing to do when given a choice, you have been one of God's angels.

God places angel wings on all of us. How they are used is determined if we realize they are there. If you use them to fly away, then you have chosen not to be one of God's angels. Being one of God's angels is not a difficult thing. It may only require a smile from you. It may only require a hug. Or it may require a simple hello to someone no one else has acknowledged. Reaching out to someone and giving of yourself is all that is needed. Do you feel the wings upon your back? It is never too late to discover them. You are God's hands, feet, and voice. Use them for His glory, and He will love you into eternity.

> And Jesus spoke to them, saying, "I am the light of the world. Whoever follows me will never walk in darkness but will have the light of life."
>
> John 8:12

To My Son

I love you, son
with all my heart,
with all my soul,
and with everything I am.
You are my today, my tomorrow
and my life.
You are perfect in my eyes
and you are perfect in my heart.
Together we can accomplish anything
and together we will see tomorrow.
With every challenge
there will be a victory;
With every victory
there will be a memory;
And with every memory
we will build your future.
I will be your greatest teacher.
Through me you will learn
how to be a friend,
how to be a father
and most importantly,
how to be a man.
Watch me, listen to me
and always trust me.

My footprints will be your guide.
I love you, son
and that will never change.

I wrote this for my son, Ryan, when he was born. I already had a beautiful daughter, Aleesha, and when she was born, she stole my heart. She still has a firm grip on it even though she is in her thirties and living miles away with her devoted husband, Matthew. I treasure both Aleesha and Matthew very much.

Having a son makes a man feel he has replaced himself on this earth. He feels if anything ever happened to him, his son would be there to care for the family. As a father, it is your responsibility to keep your children safe by teaching them the things that will do so. It is also your responsibility to not put them into situations where they will suffer shame and humiliation. It is an awesome responsibility, but it also one you treasure as a father.

Can you imagine how difficult it must have been for God to send His only Son to live a life of pain, misery, ridicule, and eventually death? As a father, He had to have felt a pain we cannot imagine. I could not have done this with any of my children.

Ryan is a paramedic. He risks his own life every day, and he saves many lives along the way. It is difficult not to worry about his safety, but I trust God to watch over him. I do not know what Ryan's future will be, but God does.

God knew what His son would face when He sent Him to earth. He knew that one day His son would die for people who would not understand. As a father, knowing this was going to happen is unimaginable.

God loves us. He proved that by sending His son to die for us. He made the ultimate sacrifice as a parent. God does not expect us to do the same as He did. All He asks is we love Him above all others and everything else. That is not a sacrifice. As a Christian, it should be a privilege.

> Children, obey your parents in the Lord, for this is right. "Honor your father and mother"—this is the first commandment with a promise: so that it may be well with you and you may live long on the earth." And, fathers, do not provoke your children to anger, but bring them up in the discipline and instruction of the Lord.
>
> Ephesians 6:1–4

> Hear, my child, and accept my words, that the years of your life may be many. I have taught you the way of wisdom; I have led you in the paths of uprightness. When you walk, your step will not be hampered; and if you run, you will not stumble. Keep hold of instruction; do not let go; guard her, for she is your life.
>
> Proverbs 4:10–13

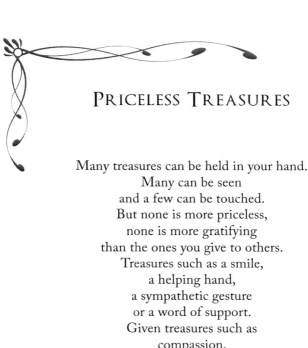

PRICELESS TREASURES

Many treasures can be held in your hand.
Many can be seen
and a few can be touched.
But none is more priceless,
none is more gratifying
than the ones you give to others.
Treasures such as a smile,
a helping hand,
a sympathetic gesture
or a word of support.
Given treasures such as
compassion,
love,
friendship,
and understanding
cannot be measured.
The giving away of these treasures
only makes you richer.
The giving away of these treasures
only reaps happiness.
The possession of these treasures
is a true sign of wealth.
Give and you shall receive.
If nothing more,
the feeling of satisfaction
because you have given of yourself.

After a baby is born, what is the one thing everyone wants to see the baby do? Smile. We go to great lengths and make the strangest noises and faces to try to get the baby to smile. Why do you think this is? It's because a smile means so much to us. It is the outward expression that lets us know someone is happy. Seeing their happiness makes us happy. We get the same feeling when someone gives us a kind word or conveys a gesture of love or friendship. These acts are gifts we crave. We live our lives wanting to be loved, respected, and noticed. We want to feel someone cares, even if it is a stranger.

God gives us so many gifts. He puts within each of us the potential to be whatever we choose to be. Along with this potential, God gives us a heart and mind that He fills with gifts meant to be given to others. They are gifts to us, but they are actually priceless treasures to others. Our willingness to share these treasures with others is up to us. We choose whether to let others see the treasures that could change their life. To do so though will require making yourself vulnerable to others. It will require you to be the first to speak, the first one to smile, the one who starts a conversation, or the one that asks if you can help. It might even require you to choose to sacrifice something in order for someone else to succeed or receive what they need. These gifts may only seem like simple gestures to you. They may seem like "the right things to do." But to someone who needs a smile, a handshake, or a kind word, they are priceless treasures.

God wants us to love each other. The golden rule applies at all times: "In everything, do to others as you would have them do to you; for this is the law and the prophets" (Matthew 6:12). I am afraid our world has begun changing the golden rule to "do unto others before they do unto you." Let's not let this happen. Reach out to others and see where you can make a difference. Jesus came to earth to show us this exact principle. Look around. The treasures you possess can be given away every day if you look for those who need them most.

For where your treasure is, there your heart will also be.

Matthew 6:21

THE GREATEST MOVEMENT

Movement of something physical
like a chair or our bodies can be seen.
Movement in music is good.
It brings out the feeling
and gives emphasis to the song.
But the most important movement of all,
the one seen every day by everyone,
the one most taken for granted,
is a silent movement.
A movement only noticed if you are looking for it.
It is the movement of an emotion.
A tear of joy.
A smile of accomplishment.
A parent's swelling pride
when a son or daughter succeeds.
The birth of a child.
The reunion with a loved one.
And the relief when it all finally fits.
These are all movements most cherished,
ones most important,
most treasured,
and longest remembered.
These are the feelings that appear
when you find yourself most paying attention.

The chills,
the lighthearted excitement—
all are not conscious, controllable emotions.
They are hidden,
never under control
and suddenly experienced.
Do you remember these emotions?
Do you have special memories because of them?
Let us never try to understand these movements of emotion.
Let us never explore for the reasons why.
Let us, for once, accept
something that comes so fast
but will live in our heart forever.

Emotions are what make life worth living. If we were devoid of emotion that would mean we could not love, create, explore, write, or speak. Emotions help us know we are alive. They help us express ourselves. They help us reach up and out to others. They give us reasons for praying. God knew what He was doing when He gave us the ability to see, touch, feel, and hear. All of these senses are what makes us know we are in love. They let us know when we are right or wrong. They let us know when we have hurt someone. But most importantly, our emotions are a part of our Christian faith.

When we think about what Christ endured on the cross, we are saddened. When we hear music speaking of the love of God, we are spiritually and emotionally moved. When we read in our Bible the answer to all of our questions, we are at peace because we know we are loved. Having emotions is essential to a good Christian life. They help us feel what we should feel, see what we should see, and love others as Jesus taught us to do.

Be open with your emotions. Be passionate about what you believe. Be emotional. Let everyone know the love in your heart, the compassion in your soul, and the reason your life is different. Christ was emotional, and through his emotions, He made a difference.

> By contrast, the fruit if the Spirit is love, joy, peace, patience, kindness, generosity, faithfulness, gentleness, and self-control. There is no law against such things.
>
> Galatians 5:22–26

GIVING OF YOURSELF

The giving of yourself is never easy.
Sometimes you're misunderstood.
Sometimes you're just overlooked.
When people give of themselves,
it is enrichment,
if not for the receiver,
then certainly for the giver.
How easily such action can be missed.
How easily it can go unnoticed.
When a child pauses and says, "I love you,"
when he makes something especially for you,
it is a portion of himself he extends to you.
Let us never become engrossed beyond the recognition of a
child.
The giving of yourself can be dangerous.
It can alienate and confuse people.
A thoughtful deed confused for charity,
a sympathetic word taken as pity,
or a helping hand taken as an intrusion—
all may have started as an extension of yourself
but ended with the creation of a void.
The giving of yourself can be wonderful and beautiful
when such action can be seen as help
and the simple response of a smile appears.

Careful thought and common sense
can sometimes prevent the sudden loss of communication.
Don't be afraid to give of yourself.
Don't let neglect turn to regret.
Just be sure you give when it is needed.
Because the giving of yourself
may not be recognized immediately by the receiver.
But one day it will be remembered, appreciated,
and never to be forgotten.

How many times have you thought of reaching out to someone in need only to then decide not to because of a fear of the gesture being misunderstood? We have all done this. That fear comes from past experiences or knowing of similar situations that did not turn out well for others. There is always the fear society and the media have placed on all of us, the fear that the person is looking for a handout and is not genuine in their need. Being compassionate and giving of yourself can be very tensive. Knowing when to open your heart to someone is never easy. Making yourself vulnerable to others can get your feelings hurt. There is an old saying that is a little jaded but it sometimes applies when you give of yourself: "No good deed ever goes unpunished." Gestures that are done with compassion in your heart and not for recognition are the ones that God sees.

When you see an opportunity to help, don't be afraid to do so. When you reach out to someone and they slap your hand away, don't be discouraged. When your actions bring you criticism from others, it will probably be because they are envious of your ability to care. Don't be swayed by the world's opinion of caring. Unfortunately, there will be times when you are genuine in your love and caring but people will still misunderstand. These times will be few, and there will be more times when you will make a difference in someone's life. Give and you shall receive. That is God's way.

> Now may our Lord Jesus Christ himself and God
> our Father, who loved us and through grace gave us
> eternal comfort and good hope, comfort your hearts
> and strengthen them in every good work and word.

> 2 Thessalonians 2:16–17

TAKING WHAT WE HAVE

Taking what we have,
using what we can,
and being what we want
are all signs of success and determination.
When we accept what we are
and don't strive for higher realms,
we become as stone—
hard and stationary.
When we stifle our growth,
we hinder our mobility.
When we limit ourselves
to small goals and accomplishments,
we become as small as our objectives.
A man can only become as large as his dreams.
Small minds produce small successes;
great and broad minds
produce everything else.
Let us not limit ourselves
because we feel we cannot excel.
Don't handicap yourself by thinking negatively.
Inferiority starts on the outside
when someone tells you that you are inferior.

But it can only grow to something true when you believe it
and accept it in your heart.
Take what God has given you
and make it a blessing to Him
every day.

When God created a man and woman, He placed them in the garden of Eden and gave them everything they would need to survive. One of the greatest gifts He gave them was the freedom to choose what they would do and not do. We refer to this as free will. Though God knew it would be a hard thing for them to do, He still allowed them to make their own decisions. It is no different now than then.

We are free to use the gifts God gave us. The choices we make will determine the direction we will go. Though there are many factors that control our direction, God gives us the ability to accomplish whatever we decide to do. When we limit ourselves to small goals and objectives, that will be exactly what we will get.

Open your mind, open your imagination and let them create your goals in life. You are a child of God. God wants your life to be great. Make it great by making it about being your best. You will be great if you believe you will be great and you prepare yourself to become great.

We must no longer be children, tossed to and fro and blown about by every wind of doctrine, by people's trickery, by their craftiness in deceitful scheming. But speaking the truth in love, we must grow up in every way into him who is the head, into Christ, from whom the whole body, joined and knit together by every ligament with which it is equipped, as each part is working properly, promotes the body's growth in building itself up in love.

Ephesians 4:14–16

INSIDE A TEAR

If you could look inside a tear
you would see what's inside a person's heart.
You will see happiness and joy
or sadness and pain.
Inside a tear
are the walls we hide behind.
We cry when we need to
and we cry when we have to.
Inside a tear you will find
the root of a person's soul.
Their loves, their hates, and their deepest fears
will slide slowly down their cheek,
eventually falling to the ground
or being wiped away
along with the reason for their tears.
Tears that we shed openly
will come and go in just moments.
But there are tears
that no one can look inside of.
These are the tears we shed
not from our eyes
but from our heart.
God allows us to embrace our tears.
God gives us moments in our life

where our tears will be our only means
to cleanse our soul.
Tears we shed openly
will give us solace at that moment.
But the tears we shed inside
are the ones that change our life
forever.

A tear is an expression of vulnerability. It is an expression of the heart when it is either smiling with joy or weeping from pain. A tear can be cleansing to our soul and still be an expression of a deep hurt that we feel will never go away. Within every tear is a story. As clear as the tear itself, the reason for the tear is easy for us to see. But sometimes the reason for the tears is confusing to others. They see the tears and feel they have caused them. Because of this, many people do not let others see them cry. We should not be concerned about the impression others have about our tears. Holding inside the fears and the hurts we all feel is never healthy. Never let your emotions be stifled by the fear of public ridicule. We all suffer, and maybe if more of us expressed emotionally the fears we feel, we would find comfort in knowing we are not alone.

God cries, I am sure. He cries when He sees us struggling. He cries when He wants to help, but we keep forgetting He is there. Jesus cried many times. His last words to His Father were said through a weeping voice, "My God, my God, why hast thou forsaken me?"

Do not be afraid of your tears. They are not a sign of weakness, but it is a sign of caring. Embrace your tears and let them wash away your sadness or help you rejoice in your happiness. God is with you always. He will never forsake you. God sees your every tear and the reason for each one as you wipe them away. He also hears your crying from within as you shed those secret tears. Pray and tell God the reason for your tears. He is always listening. You must always remember that God is love and you are loved by God.

> May those who sow in tears reap shouts of joy. Those who go out weeping, bearing the seed for sowing, shall come home with shouts of joy, carrying their sheaves.

> Psalms 126:5–6

BONUS: SEVEN-DAY PLAN

To end this book, I thought it might be nice to give you something to try. I wrote the following seven-day plan. I am practicing this, and it has helped me many times. I developed it over time by experiencing, observing, and watching the world around me. Too many times we go through our days not noticing anything around us. We don't look for the good in our lives. We don't notice the people and events that move us through our day. We make decisions based on our environment. How people treat us affects how we treat others. The actions of others, hopefully, make us think if we would act the same way given the same opportunities. Being aware of what is happening around you is important. Knowing if your behavior is genuine or if you are controlled by what happens around you is essential.

This is a seven-day plan to help change your attitude and your outlook on life and make you think more deeply about the world around you. Read the three daily questions and answer them as honestly as you can. This exercise will open your mind and change your perception of yourself and others you encounter.

Try it for seven days and see how it changes the way you perceive people, the way you perceive yourself, and how you will look at life today and in the future.

Monday

- What inspired me today?
- What moved me today?
- What surprised me today?

Tuesday

- What touched me today?
- What gave me hope today?
- What disappointed me today?

Wednesday

- What made me wonder today?
- What made me reach out to someone today?
- What humbled me today?

Thursday

- What made me angry today?
- What scared me today?
- What made me grow as a person today?

Friday

- What turned me off today?
- What new thing did I do today?
- What new memory did I create today?

Saturday

- What new friendships did I make today?
- What did I do for someone else today?
- What did I see someone else do for someone today?

Sunday

- What act of kindness did I do today?
- What Christian act did I do today?
- What wrong did I right today?